The Paths of Survival

Josephine Balmer

The Paths of Survival

Shearsman Books

First published in the United Kingdom in 2017 by
Shearsman Books
50 Westons Hill Drive
Emersons Green
BRISTOL
BS16 7DF

Shearsman Books Ltd Registered Office
30–31 St. James Place, Mangotsfield, Bristol BS16 9JB
(this address not for correspondence)

www.shearsman.com

ISBN 978-1-84861-529-8

ACKNOWLEDGEMENTS

Many of the poems in this collection have been previously published (in these
or earlier version) in the following: *Agenda, Arion, Frear* (in Greek
translations by Paschalis Nikolaou), *Long Poem Magazine, Mediterranean
Poetry, Modern Poetry in Translation, New Statesman,* and *Tellus.*
'Draughts' was written for the 'Classics and Class' project at King's College,
London. 'The Pagan's Tip' was written for 'A New Palladas' conference
at University College, London, September 2014.

For help, encouragement and support, thanks are also due to Tony Frazer,
Edith Hall and Henry Stead of the Classics and Class project, Fiona Cox,
Elena Theodorakopoulos, Johnny Marsh, W.S. Milne, the indefatigable
Paschalis Nikolaou and the ever-patient Paul Dunn.

Contents

Just as our lives can be represented as texts which we make, so our selves are inseparable from the texts we read and make our own...
   —*Charles Martindale*

Myrmidons... It didn't survive; only the title and some fragments. I would join Sisyphus in Hades and gladly push my boulder up the slope if only, each time it rolled back down, I were given a line...
   —from *The Invention of Love*, Tom Stoppard

...Weapons, we need new weapons...
   Aeschylus, *Myrmidons*

Proem: Final Sentence

(Sackler Library, Oxford, Present Day)

Still I am drawn to it like breath to glass.
That ache of absence, wrench of nothingness,
stark lacunae we all must someday face.

I imagine its letters freshly seared;
a scribe sighing over ebbing taper,
impatient to earn night's coming pleasures
as light seeped out of Alexandria.

But in these hushed corners of Oxford
Library afternoons, milky with dust,
the air is weighted down by accruing loss

and this displaced scrap of frayed papyrus
whose mutilated words can just be read,
one final, half-sentence: *Into darkness…*
Prophetic. Patient. Hanging by a thread.

Custodians

*...By absence from battle, am I not our army's
True champion?...*

The Librarians' Power
(The National Library, Baghdad, 2003)

We carried what we could to safety.

They seemed like something living:
fungus on an oak, the pleated folds
of open mushroom cup, organisms
that were once books, manuscripts,
now debris of 'precision' incendiary.

To conserve them we needed ice
not fire. In a ruined kitchen cellar
we found a freezer but no power;
we canvassed, coaxed, cajoled
until locals offered the sacrifice
of their one precious generator.

We were asked why we struggled
to save books while all around us
so many of our citizens were lost.
We could only say that, if not flesh,
here were dividing cells, bare blocks
of collective memory. Conscience.

The vast record of all our knowledge
and of our faith: an ancient Quran,
the House of Wisdom we had built;
the learning we alone had salvaged
and then protected for the Greeks –
Ptolemy's *Almagest*, science, medicine.

Those lost worlds were retrieved
in the flash of forceps, lifting piece
on tiny piece, word on broken word.
Our own enduring, unshakeable belief
that in each newly-deciphered letter
a poem waited to be recovered.

Trespass

(Monastery of Zavorda, Macedonia, 1959)

From the crag we watched as he drew
near, creeping closer like a contagion.

'My son, we have been expecting you,'
our unsmiling abbot said in welcome.
From the cadence of his voice we knew
he was not talking of days or decades
but the dry passage of our centuries.
For weeks our guest rifled the libraries,
their rare treasures piled around him –
like a child's toys or stored-up treats.

Now our abbot did not eat or sleep.
We saw the apprehension in his face
as if some half-recalled, splintered dream
had returned, long dreaded, to haunt him,
a fear he could barely form or elucidate.
Our guest found all he had come to seek:
a tattered codex wrapped round in rags
like some precious shard of brittle glass.
He put on his hat and coat, his work done,
a few more words for his literary canon –

Abdeluktos philo. Absolved because I loved him...
Anathema. The taint of unconstrained sin –
a snatch of Aeschylus' foul *Myrmidons*.
In its shadow we had held sacred homily,
called our brethren to vespers, benediction.
Now it was unleashed again, this heresy
we had guarded here without knowing
for so long. Unspeakable acts. Trespass.

We waited as he faded, a blur in the dark,
disappearing back into fold of river pass.

Excavators

...I have shaken
Out the reins, let loose the horses
To run the course of truth...

Papyrus Trace

(Papyrological Institute, Florence, 1953)

Among the professor's papers
deposited after her recent death –

calculations, petty cash registers,
even a house plan in faint sketch –

we found a pencilled transcript,
scrawled in haste, not remembered,

traced beneath an old shopping list,
a breath exhaled, deep-buried ember:

trapped in the scent of lavender, musk;
letters from a lost world, seeping back

to black, etched in breath-blown dust:
...speak out... ...dissent... ...enough...:

a few precious words of Aeschylus
we'd all believed had gone forever –

the fragment found at Oxyrhynchus
then lost again in an Allied raid

by this second miracle returned to us,
late violets trembling above a grave.

The Professor's Prize

(Florence, 23rd March 1944, p.m)

That day I'd seen a student hung
from a lamp post by a baying mob
for 'associating' with other men.
All night I sat alone, working on.
Which is where I heard it, sob
of stray, thumb-slipped bomb.
I didn't think of the house I had
just lost, not even a prayer – God
forbid – for the beloved sister
who'd shared it all these years,
(no need to panic for the husband
and children that were never there,
the family sacrificed for Greek
that hadn't filled it, never would)
this fear was for a thin glass case,
scrap of papyrus pressed between,
marbled, translucent, bled at the edge
like collector's rare butterfly wing.
The only one not in safe-keeping –
the one I'd held, could not evacuate

Later we found my sister Eugenia
barely scratched, her face at peace
as if a chance she still might speak.
No such fortune for the precious text
my murdered friend had excavated
in Egypt, brought back in triumph.
He was proud that day, possessed –
like a Greek tragic hero, we all said –
flushed with his new-found success.
And with a hero's courage to defy,
to speak up for his faith, for who
and what he was, the men he loved:
Time now to protest, to dissent...

Today all I see are his bulging eyes
and purple lips, the scar of rope,
face twisted into a scream of *No*.

He'd entrusted me with his prize
as if written in his own blood,
our own golden treasure trove
shrunk away into shrivelled cinder.
Now it was lost, alchemy in reverse,
transformed back to lead and dirt.

Itch

(Florence, 23rd March 1944, a.m.)

I felt I was a tourist or maybe even God
poised above the city's glowing sites
with power over creation, destruction –
all lost or saved in the squeeze of a knob,
history held between finger and thumb.

As we turned back, I think I sneezed
or my co-pilot twitched, an itch maybe.

I saw it fall, a grey speck on a single house.
For a moment I thought of my baby son
as smoke spiralled up like umbilical cord.
For his sake there was no time to fuss,
our mission had been achieved without loss.
Targets: both destroyed. Stray objects hit: one.
Ground casualties: not known. Job: well done.

The Student's Find

(Oxyrhynchus, Egypt, 1932)

I was only too happy to keep
my head down, hands in muck
and silt. At home in Florence,
we were pinkos, pederasts,
as the thugs waited on street
corners, ready to smash fists
in faces, ribs – or worse…
Even a former *carabiniere*
had been arrested, we heard,
sentenced to five years' *confino*,
ditto the boy he had adored –
filth, infections to be purged.

I signed up for the Institute dig
as my fellow students teased –
the most fastidious of our party
shovelling shit on his knees.
Now I watch our stout spiv
of a site director puffing past,
spotless, in his shiny spats
and striped suit, trilby cocked,
dressed for dinner not detritus.
Still, he offers a way to live:
"Politics are not my business,"
he says, "I care only for papyri."

Sometimes as I sift the pieces –
broken lives slot back into place
shrill petitions, desperate pleas;
the constant, unremitting fear,
that makes us flatter, supplicate.
And then, like the first flicker
of smoking fire, slow to take,
I found a tattered word: *Antelexa*:

My heart turned over. I knew it:
speak out. oppose. dissent.

Later there came confirmation
from the professors in Florence;
I had unearthed a precious sliver
of Aeschylus' lost *Myrmidons* –

a new sigh from a long silence:
A stifled cry shuddering back:
Enough is enough. No more slander,
no more slurs to crush the tongue.
Time now to protest, to dissent.

A point of no return. The moment
all the lies might start to shatter

Editors

…I see you all shrink back in horror…

Redaction

(John Cramer, The Royal Library, Paris, July 1834)

I barely saw the city. I tracked down
only texts for extract. But as I studied,
the Library's high windows shuddered
with the shouts of rioters – republicans,
radicals, they told us. On Rue Vivienne
the injured were stowed like receipted
books or consulted papers. One corpse
lay crumpled, a read note, in the street.
I walked on by, non-aligned. I thought
of the desk I had just left, its volumes
still untouched, smooth as fresh sheets.

Yet even here I was no longer safe.
As the hiss and boom of gunfire ceased,
I turned a leaf, easing out the crease,
leaning on my elbows for weight;
an old manuscript, deep in the collection,
a work I should never have breached:
I am absolved because I loved him –
a reference, if I was not much mistaken,
to the unspeakable vice of the Greeks.
In Aeschylus! I copied author and play
then scratched them out. Better not to say.

Draughts

(Richard Porson, Cambridge, 1795)

I drank to make it go away, the Greek
I thought in, dreamt in, that slurred my speech
far more than village burr I was born with –
the farm boy who had conquered Cambridge.
I took six jugs of port before breakfast;
at dinner, wine, ink, dregs of fellow-guests.

But still my drowned memory did not fail.
I still knew Lucian's *Erotic Tales*
backwards, could read each word with closed eyes;
there I found it, Aeschylus' line of vice –
such sacred communion between the thighs –
his great heroes no more than sodomites.

Unshrinking, I added it to my draughts,
attributed the text, a thankless task.
They said I hiccupped Greek like a helot,
spewed out sewer English. Stipends
were withheld by outraged college patrons,
promised professorships suddenly lost.

They thought I should abstain, the idiots.
I was mulched from Norfolk soil, sky-soaked stock.
And we all sip from the same poisoned pot.

It was knowledge now, could not be forgot.

Scavengers

...This is the sweat of war, the way it is;
We all pay the price of your politics...

Hoard

(Giovanni Aurispa, Constantinople & Venice, 1423)

In the Bazaar I bartered shirt and sword,
careful its hawkers did not sense the worth
of the books they had piled up as if soiled.
For here was the hoard of forgotten worlds,
discoloured texts as dark as clouded pearls.

Back home, I caressed my acquisitions,
tenderly, afraid their soft skin might tear.
I had no lovers, I knew no passion
except for this, for words. My life's breath. Air.

Yet it seemed I cradled Bosphorus sand
that slipped through my fingers. Or drifts of snow
from the peaks of Parnassus, Pelion,
shrunk in a second by our Venice sun,
no more than water trickling through the hand.

The Clerk's Crusade

(Constantinople, 12th April 1204)

The first thing we noticed was mortar
crumbling, sand trickling from a stone.
Even rats, the Captain shrugged, get restless
under siege, gnawed by our same hunger.
The guards returned to their next throw
of dice. And I slunk back to Library desk.

We could not know, did not even guess
our city was already falling, already ash.

Next day we all saw it, the slab shift
and slowly tilt. We stood transfixed
as a single block of wall rolled back
and chasm opened where it collapsed;
ten withered fingers gripped the edge,
then Crusader helmet on Crusader head.
Our captain gave orders. On cue we fled.

That night Byzantium was melted down.
Everything they could move, they took.
All else was toppled into steaming pots,
vast statues shrunk to stumps of bronze,
for each piece of tessera, another life lost.

Myself, I looted what they overlooked.

As Latin bishops stripped our churches
of jewels, I stuffed my splattered jerkin
with a few foxed and battered books:
Photius' *Lexicon*, Lucian, Athenaeus.
Here was no Holy War but Christian
against Christian, West against East.
Better the Saracens. They had belief.

I ran back through the streets, slipping
on spilt blood, fresh excrement, filth.
Far off, a woman sobbed, out of reach.
I squeezed out through the breach,
a conqueror in reverse. For in Nicaea
or the monasteries of Thessalonica,
we would soon found another empire.

Our nobles crept away like thieves
as the Latins jeered, waving inkpots,
quills – the weapons not of warriors
but meek scholars, they hissed.

                    Let them mock.

Where they had cruelty, we had culture.
Where they had greed, we had Greek.

Translators

...I see no disgrace in voicing
Such words...

Gerard's Constellations
(Southern Spain, 1175)

I came to Toledo to map the stars.

I was hunting Ptolemy's *Almagest*,
the key to our crammed skies, held safe
there all these centuries by the Moors.
Its charts, I heard, steered men homewards
through ink-black seas, night's vastness,
constellations tracked as if by a thread.

Now I saw it all, sphere on sphere
worlds opening up, unlocked doors –
catalogued, fixed, holding us here.

After the skies I discovered the earth:
medicine, mathematics, the healing works
of the Greeks, studded with metaphor,
a science that glittered like poetry.

So I translated them, last in a chain –
Greek to Arabic and now my Latin –
striving to be faithful yet make them sing.

But alone at night I found myself dreaming
of other, unknown poets; the anguish
of their words drifting out into darkness,
as if sailors becalmed by unfamiliar waters
with no way back when the daylight falters.
And, in cloud, stars are slowly extinguished,
dimming, one by one, before they vanish.

Hunayn's Gold

(The House of Wisdom, Baghdad, 860)

He is putting us out of business.

By translating the texts of the Greeks
into Arabic, he has stripped us Syrians,
Christians, of all our physicians' secrets.

What's worse, we heard that he was paid
by weight; for each piece of parchment
he piles up gold. Hippocrates and Galen
are now inscribed on the thickest vellum,
double-spaced, in round discursive script
for every word in Greek, two in Arabic –
the more the pages, the more the payment.

Yes, Hunayn ibn Ishaq will know regret.

We watch him as he caresses his works,
balancing up their worth, word by word.
But he needs to remember his position;
he is a mere translator, not a physician –
a swordsmith does not wield the sword.
He must heed the proverb of the Greeks:
the weapons by which we are vanquished
come not from others but our own wings.
Yes, Hunayn should take care. His inks,
like gold, are precious, envied, dangerous.
So we have denounced him to the Caliph.

His prized Library will be confiscated
and he himself disgraced, condemned –
punishment for the crimes he perpetrated.
But still he is unrepentant, still shameless:
'You fools,' he gasps, defiant to the end,
'you only see the gold in your own grasp.

I translate the books that require to be read:
precious works deserve exquisite materials.
This is the way I will ensure their survival.'

Let him spit. We have had our revenge.
Our knowledge will be safe from theft.
He can write all he likes of cures and health.
We own the wisdom that brings us wealth.

Victors

…When you hear
The clash of battle, of slaughter,
When you hear of men suffering
Why do you not come to their aid?…

Gloss

(Photius I, Byzantium, 858)

I worked my way up by my wits, from clerk
to city Patriarch. I corrected
each schism, effaced the iconoclasts
until our gilded streets turned black. And red.

In broken churches we counted the deaths.
I remembered a reed-slim boy of nine
or ten, the taste of his salt lips on mine –
weed-choked detritus dragged from Golden Horn.

Now terms were defined in my Lexicon.
I started with alpha: **Abdeluktos**
Above blame. Any heretics tortured,
maimed. *Absent of guilt*. All Jews slaughtered.
[æb'dɛl'uk'tɒs] A sword hissing through bone.
Absolved. Assaults washed clean by each fresh gloss.

Amr's Last Words

(Fustat, Egypt, 664)

That night earth crept close to heaven
and I was crushed between, breathing
in through eye of a needle, unafraid
now, the stilled voice of a dying man.
Around my tented couch, the deserts
I had subdued stretched out, oblivious;
stars inked new scripts on dulled skies
as my life shrunk to sand speck, dust.
I remembered Alexandria, possessing
a city of 4,000 palaces & 4,000 baths,
400 marble theatres, 200 greengrocers
& 1 Library. I heard how the Ptolemies
filled the shelves with borrowed books,
confiscated 'tax' from anchored ships,
instructing their scribes to copy works
in secret, returning only the duplicates.
I had to choose which to save and which
to burn. Those that spoke of God I kept,
the rest, as ordered, went in the furnace.

The tragedies of the Greeks were first.
I can hear the crack of curled papyrus,
still smell that acrid, smouldering ash.

You ask what death tastes like. It is this.

Believers

...You must do whatever you think right...

The Christians' Cheek
(Alexandria, 391)

We're old hands these days,
true believers for decades –
apart, of course, for the break
effected by Julian the Apostate
(when we found it was politic
to revert – just for the interim –
to blood rites, full sacrifice).
Now we've changed back again.

Our new emperor Theodosius
has outlawed all pagan practice,
that tribe of soothsayers, seers;
all the priests of Thoth, Serapis,
trite dramatists, epigrammatists
with their sharp-tongued sneers.
We'll storm their prized Libraries,
strip the dwindling shelves bare.
Who needs poetry or philosophy
when you have faith, orthodoxy?

For we are so tired of turning
the other cheek; time to shed ink,
shred parchment. It's a while since
we've put a knife to fine calf-skin.

The Pagan's Tip

(Oxyrhynchus, Upper Egypt, 390)

Today we sacrificed our last bull —
not easy, with just the five of us.
Walking back with Kallas, my cousin,
we both agreed it was time to stop.
Now, we said, we are all Christians.

That night I gathered up the volumes
my family had prized over the years:
philosophy, poetry, the great dramas
of Aeschylus, epigrams of Palladas —
texts our ancestors had brought home
in triumph from each trip to Alexandria.

Those pages hold our history like maps.
If I run my fingers over the covers,
their gold letters and tooled leather,
I can trace the twisted paths of our past.
This is who we were and what we are:
grammarians, clerks, petty bureaucrats.

On the shelf I replaced each space
with Paul's *Epistles*, all the *Gospels*.
Ours I took out beyond the walls
among the flies and rotting waste,
left them there for the rats to soil
like any piece of discarded refuse.

Do the same, if you want my advice.

Emperor

... Think of the men betrayed, spear fodder,
Sacrificed while their own commander
Sulks, safe in his tent ...

Entrenchment

(Caracalla, Alexandria, 215)

We'd heard the rumours, knew his bad report,
still we welcomed him with music, torches,
threw petals under his feet as he walked:
the emperor known as 'cut-price Oedipus'
(he'd killed his brother to marry mother) –
we Alexandrians love gossip, satire.

Now he styled himself the new Achilles,
summoned our young men as his own phalanx.
We sneered in secret at his vanities
as they lined for parade, dug trench on trench.
Yet still we watched in pride, picked out our own –
a flash of hair or cloak as they worked on.

Slumped over Aeschylus' *Myrmidons* –
I have heard so many insolent threats –
Caracalla skulked in the Serapeum.
And then scent of earth became stench of flesh.
From afar he gave the signal to slay
our sons. Then we knew; they'd dug their own graves

and so had we. From afar we saw dead
packed on dead, rising in burial mounds,
some pushed in alive, crushed, suffocated.
Back in our gates, he placed armed guards around
each quarter, walled us up in our own streets,
burned our books, destroyed our academies.

How many killed I neither care nor know –
only that each last one deserved to die,
his wrote in his dispatches back to Rome.
For now the city has been purified.
He sacrificed cows to our temple gods
as he'd sacrificed us to his own wrath.

The jokes were over. We renamed him 'the Beast' –
a title he earned, role he revelled in.
We had thought we were such sophisticates,
shielded by our wit, our erudition,
safe in our city's shining walls, aloof.
He dyed them black with the blood of our youth.

Anthologists

…Let me honour
Our passion, such sacred communion
Between the thighs…

Erotic Tales

(Lucian, Samosata, Syria, 200)

I'd thought of myself as the new Homer.

But readers, I soon learnt, prefer horror,
sci-fi. My *Erotic Tales* pay the bills,
bring in the hard cash, the boys and/or girls.
Even Aeschylus, known for weighty verse,
dipped his nib in the ambidextrous:
such sacred communion between the thighs
sighed his Achilles over pert backside
to top my list of things bi-curious.

And who's to say I'm not as lyrical?
Across the empire, at any scribe's stall,
my 'lightweight' prose is still copied ten times
more than dull, turgid tragedies. Is this
a talent wasted? Or career waylaid?
Weighty or not, they'll remember my lines
when Aeschylus' plays have long decayed.

Supper Sophistries

(Athenaeus, Naucratis, c.200)

I dine on extracts, a small talk supper
sophist, drinking-party philosopher.
I pepper titbits and sauce anecdotes,
reduce our tragic verse to bite-size quotes.

Though now it seems I'm gutting carrion,
stripping the off cuts from some rotted corpse,
scouring for scraps to season. Or to poach.
Until, because of me, mere crumbs remain.

Yet these sustain. My specks of Aeschylus
will stew in the pot, rise above the scum
like precious spices or gold-flecked amber
lavish eastern cooks might pare for garnish –
my love, remember all the nights we shared…

The aftertaste that lingers on the tongue.

Scribe

...Grieve for me now...

Blot

(Alexandria, 150)

It barely matters if I blot or blotch –
these days no one asks for Aeschylus.

As light fades I head for the streets –
a cheap tavern or the house of whores –
to scrub off this stain of guilt and remorse,
flaws that cling like yesterday's rotten fish.
On mornings after, I retake my seat,
propping up each eyelid with stylus tip,
making errors I can later edit...

And then today, a buyer for my script –
some pompous provincial bureaucrat
up from Oxyrhynchus with cold, hard cash
(although he couldn't tell drama from dog shit
all he cares is how it looks on the shelf).

For him I etch these words of love and grief.
I think of my wife, dead after a few weeks;
there'd been a baby, some complication,
the pockmarked physician couldn't tell which.
I came back one night and she was gone.

Into darkness... The skin I, too, must live in.
Mistakes uncorrected, holding the blame.

The only words left now to mask the pain.

Annotators

...The weapons by which we are vanquished
Come not from others but our own wings...

Margin

(Didymus 'Chalcenterus', Alexandria, 20 BCE)

In this line of work
you have to make
things small, short.
So I digest the refs,
pin down each taut
twist of grammar
or some rare idiom,
poetry's last crumbs -
swallow them whole
(it's not for nothing
I'm called 'Iron-guts')
then spit them all out.
Well, all except jokes.
Now I have to decipher
the so-called 'comedies'
of vulgar Aristophanes.
It's no laughing matter:
you need to annotate
every last, single letter –
the text is crude, obscure.
Still I am never sure
what's quite so jocular.
My fellow Scholiasts
try to help, to translate:
they point out puns
and double entendres.
See, they say, a tragic
chorus of Aeschylus
has become a comic
ditty, satirical rhyme.
Just call it: 'parody'.
Parody. Hmm. Poor
imitation you'll find,
the desperate remedy
of the uninspired, bereft
of anything else left
to say for themselves.
And then yesterday
a few colleagues read
a 'new' commentary
they said they'd found
for me. Immediately
I disagreed on almost
every point. They said

nothing just sniggered
behind their hands -
until they confessed
the points were mine,
all cobbled together
from my own footnotes.
I had a new name:
'Forget-What-Wrote'.
If that was a joke
I still didn't get it.
For here on the edge,
I said, there's always
a margin of error.
That just made them
laugh even more.
Aristophanes has
a lot to answer for.

Diple

(Julius Caesar, Alexandria, 48 BCE)

'Remember now and then to score the page,'
my boyhood tutor said. 'A place to return

to in the future in case you need to amend
or find a reading at first unseen, hidden;

we never know what we might miss or pass
and cannot guess. In Greek we call this *Diple*

(to rhyme with 'slip there'). Meanings are many
and move all the time. So we etch our draft.'

>>>>   <<<<<

I thought no more of it. My history was written,
achievements recorded, definitive, third person.

But then, in Alexandria, I felt the ground shift:
It was clear all were set on war with Caesar...

I saw my enemies close, the scorch of defeat.
That night it was my idea to fire the ships.

We watched the sails, huge white sparks
drifting slowly across from harbour to docks –

God-sized charcloth to catch the stores
of copied books, our whole world in draft,

stack on stack, waiting to be sent back.
Next the Library itself, illuminating the dark.

In the morning we found a smouldering gap.
The space where I could make my own mark.

Bureaucrats

...I have no sweet songs, no clever charms
To place their spell on you...

The Ferryman's Roll

(Alexandria, c.245 BCE)

The lads tease me, call me Charon. I row
out to anchored ships at night, take my tax
as ferryman, not of pennies but texts,
as our Law decrees, seizing poems, plays
for transcribing in our new Musaeum,
swearing to return all works I 'borrow'.

Last week I took some rolls of Aeschylus
to Callimachus our famed Librarian:
gilt horse-cockerel mastheads, we read, perplexed,
crafted with care, are melting, drip by drip,
in the corrosive fires of burning ships…
We joked how they must drink, these Athenians.

Callimachus did not laugh. It was fate
he said: here were the Greek prows at Troy, torched
as Achilles sulked. *Myrmidons.* Lines thought
so precious that he would not give them back.
We all groaned, aghast. Not more horse-cocks.

And then I glanced at Callimachus's face
caught in a shifting taper as he talked –
like a city put to flame, molten wax
about to twist the world into new shapes.

Reverse

(Zenon, Philadelphia, Egypt, 250 BCE)

Every day they arrive, these fresh petitions:
land titles, unpaid debts, stolen pig swill,
petty disputes over dung provisions.

Still, as everyone said, it *was* promotion.

Now I am the Minister's right-hand man,
high clerk of vast estates, acquisitions,
with a share in a boat, small plot of land.
I lay down justice, arrange state visits,
root out petty lies, expose small deceits;
I regulate beans, procure pickled fish,
cost palace furnishings, chase each receipt.

And here I have set my sights on status
and wealth, will secure my own position.

Once I arranged for a learned authority
to lecture on Homer, a good audience –
if I did have to bribe them for attendance.
Yes, I've a speck of learning on my sleeve;
I mourned my pet dog in strict elegiacs.
And in Alexandria, at Ptolemy's court,
I handled the books of the Athenians,
their potent words like lingering perfume.

Sometimes now as I tally up my takings,
the stars scratched on unrolling horizons,
numberless, through skies like torn papyrus,
I dream of Greece, Mysia's cool streams.
And find myself scribbling on the reverse
a line or two, maybe from Aeschylus;
as Achilles, war-scarred, in *Myrmidons*,
cried out at last: *We need new weapons.*

Copyists

…remember the nights we shared…

Sarpedon's Version

(Athens, 336 BCE)

When the call came from Athens for copyists,
scribes, I signed up at once; after two decades
still no one knew my name, I'd still not made it.
Even that tyrant Dionysus took first prize,
although his play had been greeted with hisses
and Diomedes, my boy, cried corruption –
we knew the charlatan had bribed the judges.
Diomedes' reward was to lose his tongue
and eyes, have the nose slashed from his bronzed face.

For all these sad years since I have guided him,
bathed him, gently walked beside at his own pace.
A few weeks ago I led him to a cliff;
the Sicilian sea below was a mirror
to hold the beauty of the world he had lost
and further out, in the dark, all its terror.
I whispered in his ear then let him step off,
the last three words we needed to hear or speak.
He could never have made the journey to Greece.

These days I transcribe Aeschylus word for word –
punishment, perhaps, for all the times we sneered,
sold his 'desk' to deluded despots, undeterred
by threat of retribution, we never once felt fear.
Lycurgus the archon guards my hunched lines,
ensuring each stroke of stylus is correct;
Athens must have control, literature defined,
the one, the only authoritative text.
And so I volunteered for the *Myrmidons* –

the fury of love lost, the blunt rage of hurt:
My love, my love, remember the nights we shared…
But even here I still dream, still have a plan,
I still believe there is time to make my mark.

I slip in lines, for myself, for Diomedes,
without shame now, our passion declared.
Now I am the hero, grief-struck Achilles –
yes, Achilles sighing to his Patroclus:
Soon I will follow you into darkness...

Aeschylus' Desk

(Sicily, 370 BCE)

That summer we posed as his heirs, brothers
fallen on hard times, hawking salvaged flotsam
as the dramatist's 'desk', still scored, so we said,
with those wild, strange words – the language
of an unknown world. This tyrant, this Dionysius,
dripping in gold and cruelty, misplaced aspiration,
bought it at once for his new Temple of the Muses –
as if he could (as if!) become a poet by association.

We spent half our talents that night in a tavern,
drinking dark Sicilian wine, warm as blood.
The rest would keep us through the winter,
myself and my 'brother', my lover Sarpedon.
In those Syracuse mornings we wrote together,
bold new verse to surpass even the Athenians.
The nights – ah, the nights were for pleasure;
I can see his reed-thin body darting out of bed

to close the shutters against October showers,
falling back into my arms like a lightning flash,
his skin sharp as thyme, the tang of turquoise sea.
Yes, History would know our names at last:
Sarpedon of Rhegium and Diomedes of Gela.
As for Dionysius, he was never a player;
to tread these barbed paths, possess poetry,
you have to let go pride, relinquish power.

Comedian

…Are [our leaders] more heroic,
Better men than I?…

Thread

(Aristophanes, Athens, 392 BCE)

Suddenly my jokes were wearing thin.

Our allies had deserted us. Even the bankers were on their knees. We melted down our temple gold for a war we could no longer end or win. And still our leaders refused to sue for peace.

> *Cry for the living not for the dead*
> *Everything we had is lost…*

For decades we had resolved disputes with words. But outside in our marbled winter streets bitterness turned to blood, flicker to fire. Rioters' shouts fell like stone in the frost-hard air. Yet we did not listen. Or include. Or appease. We would not let go so could not hold.

> *Cry for the living not for the dead*
> *Everything we had is lost…*

Defeat became inevitable. This new world required new heroes. I wrote what I could. I partied hard, aimed high, struck low. I raised the ghosts of our lost poets, the gods of our craft who had tallied up the loss of constant warfare. Who had dreamt a city that never failed or fell. Who could still walk each bone-strewn path and negotiate us back from Hell:

> *Cry for the living not for the dead*
> *Everything we had is lost…*

By taking the piss I saved the day. For years I had teetered on the line; time on time I had mocked their wild refrains and knotted epithets. Now, through my satire, they lived again. And I became the thread by which those last lines could hang:

> *Cry for the living not for brain-dead*
> *Demagogues who sit in government*
> *Fiddling expenses while cities burn.*
> *Everything they say will cost…*

But for all of us the laughter fades. Soon we will be the same – parodied and parody, tormentor and tormented, the lost and the saved – consigned to the margin of the page. We walk together into the pyre:

Cry for the living not for the dead
Everything we had is lost...

Tragedian

...What is easier to approach than death
Which men call the healer, the physician
That cures all ills?...

Aeschylus' Revision

(Gela, Sicily, 456 BCE)

I have been trying to find a word
for the colour of the sea; wind-stirred
for days now, storm-faded, foam-
flecked, shadowed by the span of egret
wings, nosing north, heading home.
But it would take a lifetime to capture
and, as my Syrian physician concurs,
I have only a fraction of one left.
And Greek is too vague, the language
of the colour blind. *Chloros.* We use it
both of rain-drenched summer grass
and sun-blanched autumn straw ('Or piss,'
as the physician notes with relish).
If we Athenians ever need to evaluate,
variegate, differentiate, we must do it
by association, metaphor, epithet –
spray-whitened, blood-raged, death-dark –
the complex adjectives my critics
have long reviled for their strangeness;
the reason, perhaps, we are at heart
a nation of politicians, tricksters, poets,
trying to catch the fleeting, the imprecise
through our tongue's own imprecision,
those dark words scarring pale papyrus
but as we write a world bursts in to light.

* * * *

Back in Athens, I know, eyebrows
have been raised. There are murmurs
I have lost my reason with my soul,
the great democrat now among tyrants.
And I have to admit that when I found
'stipend: 10 talents' – I'm not proud –

etched across the dispatch from Gela,
another world moved into focus; vibrant,
vivid, not of fame or leisure or even luxury,
but more of space, time, opportunity.
Now I have come here not to create
but to revise, to rescore, to chisel away
the features of a life's work, scrape
off the layers of accumulated dust
from the shrivelled skin of my plays:
actors always want to build their part,
add in a line or two, make speeches longer;
chorus managers, the bankers, the money-
men, will try to dictate the course of art.
And then there is the lead weight
of public opinion, the sudden hush
of an audience as a play takes shape
or the muffled coughing, the shuffled feet,
when a line misfires or speech is fluffed,
the waiting dramatist, stone-struck, aware
of the slightest change in breath or beat,
fighting the urge to rewrite then and there
(in Athens we might live by committee
but not yet, thank Gods, compose poetry).
And slowly, stealthily, intricate threads
are dropped and a work's fragile integrity,
held as if a hesitant final breath, shatters
like a vase slipping from the hands
into a thousand, thousand fragments.

* * * *

I had planned to start with *Persians* –
my version of the war I'd helped to win
against barbarism, the death of civilisation.
But as the days shrink to my writing desk,
I find myself drawn now to *Myrmidons*,
the tragedy of pride, the tragedy of passion,

the heartbeat away we are from loss:
Achilles, the warrior who will not fight,
Patroclus, the lover he will sacrifice –
the one thing he needs to live, the cost
of those dried kisses, one small slight.
Who had to learn, like the rest of us,
that flesh never returns to the skeleton,
there is no coming back from Acheron…
I had not opened it for all these years –
the sharp taunts of its harshest critics
still sting, still reverberate in the ear.
They hated my tragic hero. Speechless
and veiled throughout its early scenes,
at first no actor would agree to play him.
I had to flatter, plead, bribe, cajole:
think of the shock, I begged, the thrill
when those first words finally ring out,
reverberate around the auditorium
like lightning, a sudden flash, sparking
from seat to seat, stone row to row.
(I reminded them how, at Marathon,
the order had come round to quiet us;
to stifle our battle cries as we ran
towards the Persians, to conserve
each last breath for the coming fight).
In those days I believed my work
could still cure our diseased world;
that words had the power to change
the old order. That I could write tyranny
into democracy, transform revenge
into justice, take away our every hurt.
That if you lost a love it could be found
between the creases of unrolled papyrus.
That each flaw could somehow salve itself,
providing someone paid the sacrifice.
But to create the healing I had
to create the horror too – the Furies

who would become the Eumenides,
the Kindly Ones; the bloodshed
that could be washed away, crimes
that could be atoned for. Now here it is,
unshrinking, indelible, for all time.

* * * *

If you lost a love… As I stare across
the bay, scything my way through faded
lines I had long given up on, stylus
sharper even than a hero's blade,
all I can see is another unvoiced colour –
another blurred *chloros*: a pair of eyes
turning to mine that day in the agora
we heard how those vast Persian armies
were now on their way to destroy us;
a young man's eyes, the eyes of a warrior
as pale and soft as the last few cornflowers
at the very end of summer. Cynaegirus.
'Find strength,' he said. 'Cities can fall
in the flash of a sword but faith, ideas,
take root like weeds in its shattered halls –
there is nothing now for us to fear.'
As Athens waited, all those months,
we shared one flesh, one skin, one breath.
When the storm came, we stood together
for those ten, never-ending August nights
at Marathon, life's blood, shield-brothers,
armed against the moment the fight
would finally begin. Now the piked plain
was indivisible from sea, shields glistening
like sun-dipped waves. Time was suspended,
a sigh exhaled, trapped like a feather
between the rounds of ocean boulders.
Later, stars clashed across the skies, Orion
leading the charge, bow strung, the Hunter.

Trapped beneath, I thought of Achilles,
of all those other young men at Troy
on another plain by another blooded sea,
who knew their lives might not be long.
At last the signal came to march, destroy;
Cynaegirus at my side, we reached the ships.
his eyes in mine in the heat of battle.
Yet I hesitated, felt my knees buckle,
as the fear that Homer coloured *chloros*
like stagnant water – dank, death-gripped –
took its clammy hold. Cynaegirus
did not falter. Smiling, he stepped up
to take my place. They said he fought
like a rabid beast: *when the enemy struck,*
on all sides like wolves scattering lambs,
who strapped his shield on slender arms
and single-handedly drove them home?
Who saved you? …And then he was gone,
flesh cut to pieces, life-thread cut short.
There is no coming back from Acheron…

* * * *

Afterwards, numb, I wrote *Myrmidons*,
never able to admit it was for him
struggling to give my Achilles words.
I thought I was moving through the years
letting my work dictate my life. Was it
always the other way round? The fears
that shadowed my youth are gone.
I am no longer concerned with the death
of the body only the death of the work.
My epitaph is written: *Here lies a man*
who fought at Marathon. My plays
will tell the rest, flesh-stripped bones.
A few weeks ago I dismissed the Syrian,
words now are my only physician,

from the horror comes the healing.
Poetry flourishes in the cracks of lies,
in the white spaces between the lines –
the place I dreamed my city into being
not of gold or marble but of iron Law,
where men must account for the killing.
Where *chloros* may be the colour of fear
but also of sky, sea, a pair of pale eyes.
I take out my stylus and begin to strike;
now I must emend, I must speak out,
acknowledge to myself, to the living
and to the dead, if they still care or listen:
my love, remember all the nights we shared.
What matters now is what survives;
what time corrodes and what it spares.

Epilogue: Aeschylus' *Myrmidons* [1]
(The Surviving Text, Cambridge, Massachusetts & London, Present Day) [2]

Scene: The interior of Achilles' hut among the Greek army encampment on the beach at Troy. To one side Achilles himself sits silent and still, his face obscured from the audience; he is sulking after his argument with the Greek commander-in-chief, Agamemnon over the Trojan captive, Briseis. As the drama begins, the Chorus of Achilles' Myrmidon soldiers approaches centre stage, begging their leader to rejoin the battle.

CHORUS:

> ...Do you see, Achilles –
This is the sweat of war, the way it is;
We all pay the price of your politics.
Think of the men betrayed, spear fodder,
Sacrificed while their own commander
Sulks, safe in his tent...[3]

> ...Achilles, when you hear
The clash of battle, of slaughter,
When you hear of men suffering
Why do you not come to their aid?...[4]

Unable to goad Achilles into reacting or even speaking, the Myrmidons send for his former tutor, Phoenix.

PHOENIX:
I have no sweet songs, no clever charms
[To place their spell on you.] I have shaken
Out the reins, let loose the horses
[To run the course of truth.] Achilles,
You must do whatever [you think right...]

After Phoenix has finished his appeal, Achilles stands up and moves centre stage to face him, breaking his silence at long last.

[1] Known as 'the father of tragedy', the Athenian dramatist Aeschylus (c.525-456 BCE) was the author of about 80 plays, of which only seven now survive. These include his early work, *Persians*, which draws on his experiences as a young man in defending Athens against the Persian invasion at the battle of Marathon in 490 BCE. The tyrant Hiero of Syracuse later invited Aeschylus to revive *Persians* in Sicily where, on a subsequent visit, Aeschylus is said to have died in 456 BCE. His lost play, *Myrmidons*, famous in antiquity for its portrayal of the tragic love between the Greek hero Achilles and his fellow warrior Patroclus, was not so fortunate, with only a handful of tiny fragments remaining from a variety of sources over the ages.

[2] For a Greek text see Alan H. Sommerstein, *Aeschylus: Fragments* (2008:134-49).

[3] This fragment is contained on a papyrus fragment excavated at Oxyrhynchus, Egypt (Oxyrhynchus Papyrus 2163 frag.1). Line 1 here is also quoted by Aristophanes *Frogs* l.992, and identified as *Myrmidons* by a later Scholiast on that text.

[4] Quoted by Aristophanes, *Frogs*, ll.1264-5, and identified by a later Scholiast on that text.

ACHILLES:

...Aged [Phoe]nix, my revered advisor,
I have heard so [many] insolent th[reats]
But enough is enough. I have stayed
Silent [for too lo]ng. No more [slurs
to crush the tongue. No more slander].
Time now to protest, to dissent.[5]

[Achilles is further outraged by a report that, if he continues to refuse to fight, the Greeks will put him to death as a traitor.[6]

ACHILLES:

They say I deserve to be stoned? Do not think,
Even if pounded by r[oc]ks, that I [will weaken
My resolve]. [Remember,] how the Trojans –
And Troy – [will prosp]er without my spear...
[For wh]at is easier [to approach] than death
[Which] men call the healer, the physician
[That cures all ills]? Should[fear of] the Greeks
Send me back, spear in hand, to a war I left
In anger at its custodians. [And so] if I alone,
As our allies claim, [can do harm] to so many
By absence from battle, [am I not] our army's
True champion? [I see] no disgrace in voicing
[Such words]: are [our leaders] more heroic,
Better men than I? When [the enemy] struck
On all sides [like wolves] scattering [lambs,]
Who strapped his shield on slender arms
And single-handedly drove them [home]?
Who [saved you?]...][7]

As Achilles still refuses to fight, a message comes that the Trojans have taken the opportunity to break through Greek lines and set fire to their ships.

MESSENGER:

Look: [our] gilt horse-cockerel [mastheads],
Crafted with care, are melting, drip by drip,
In the corrosive fires [of burning ships...][8]

[5] This fragment comes from the same Oxyrhynchus papyrus as above (Oxyrhynchus Papyrus 2163 frag.11. See note 3), and is also known from a fragment excavated by an Italian team in 1932 (*Papiri della Società Italiana* ['PSI'] 1472), which was later housed in Florence. This latter fragment, which is the only copy to provide the left hand side of the text, was destroyed in an Allied air raid on the city in 1944. It was thought lost again but a transcript was discovered among the papers of Girolamo Vitelli, director of the Papyrological Institute at Florence until 1935, and of his successor, Medea Norsa, whose own house was destroyed in the raid of 1944. After her death, this was later published.

[6] The following speech – and dramatic incident – derives from a papyrus discovered by the Italian team at Oxyrhynchus (PSI 1211) although its attribution to *Myrmidons* has been disputed by many scholars (in addition, Oliver Taplin argues that it is probably not even by Aeschylus (*Harvard Studies in Classical Philology*, 76, 1972: 57-97)).

[7] Increasingly illegible, the papyrus continues in the same vein for c. 20 lines or so.

[8] Quoted by Aristophanes, *Peace*, l.1177, and *Frogs* l.932, and identified by a later Scholiast on the text.

Taking advantage of Achilles' absence from battle, the Trojans advance on the Greek lines. Achilles' lover Patroclus fights in his place, only to be killed by the Trojan hero Hector. Antilochus, the son of Nestor, brings the news back to Achilles who is distraught.

ACHILLES:
Grieve for me now, Antilochus,
Cry for the living not for the dead.
Everything we had is lost...[9]

Patroclus' body is recovered from battle and brought back to Achilles who addresses his dead lover.

ACHILLES:
How could you forget the solemn bond
We forged together, thigh wrapped
Around thigh? How could you show
Such ingratitude for all those kisses,
Endless, countless... [My love, my love,
Remember all the nights we shared...][10]

        ...Let me honour
Our passion, such sacred communion
Between the thighs; let me mourn
[All the bliss we knew together...][11]

[...For soon I will follow you do]wn
Into darkn[ess]...[12]

Achilles now cradles Patroclus' lifeless corpse.

[I see you all shrink back in horror]
Yet for me, there is no stain, no sin –
I am absolved because I loved him...[13]

In the final scene of the play, Achilles reflects on his own role in the tragedy; how his pride and stubbornness have led to his lover's death...

⁹ Quoted by Aristophanes, *Assemblywomen*, ll.392-3, and identified by a later Scholiast on the text.

¹⁰ Quoted by Athenaeus, *Supper Sophistries*, 13.602e.

¹¹ Quoted by Lucian, *Erotic Tales*, 54, although he does not gives the author and play, presumably because both were so well known at the time. These were later identified by Richard Porson in 1795.

¹² A reading of a fragmented line from a papyrus excavated at Oxyryhnchus (Oxy-rhynchus Papyrus 2256 frag. 55) which also appears to contain this speech. It is now housed in the Sackler Library, Oxford.

¹³ The line is quoted in Photius' *Lexicon* (a33), as well as subsequently cited by several later grammarians.

ACHILLES:
Remember the fable they tell in Libya
How an eagle, struck by an arrow, saw
He had been flighted by a feather and said:
'The weapons by which we are vanquished
Come not from others but our own wings.'[14]

As the play ends, Achilles prepares to go out to meet Hector in battle to avenge Patroclus' death.

ACHILLES:
Weapons, we need new weapons…[15]

[14] These lines are quoted in many works over the ages including scientific and medical tracts, many of which survived after being translated into Arabic in Syria or the libraries of Baghdad. These then came back to western Europe via the Moors of southern Spain, where scholars translated them from Arabic into Latin.

[15] The fragment's attribution to *Myrmidons* is disputed.

*...I have stayed
Silent for too long...*

Historical Notes and Sources

FINAL SENTENCE
Oxyrhynchus Papyrus 2256 contains nearly 90 scraps of papyrus; of these, number 55 is a barely legible, five-line piece, although its words could read '*kata skoton*' or 'into darkness'. It is thought these words might be part of the lover's lament Achilles murmurs over Patroclus' dead body in *Myrmidons*, later quoted by Lucian (See '*Erotic Tales*'). The fragment also appears in 'Blot' and 'Sarpedon's Version'.

THE LIBRARIANS' POWER
Inspired by an article by Zainab Bahrani with photographs by Roger LeMoyne in *Document* (Spring/Summer 2013).

TRESPASS
An account of the discovery of a previously unknown, complete new edition of the 9th century *Lexicon* of Photius by a visiting scholar at the Monastery of Zavorda, Macedonia in 1959 can be found at http://www.roger-pearse.com/weblog/2011/01/15/the-lexicon-of-photius/. Photius and his *Lexicon* also appear in 'Gloss'.

PAPYRUS TRACE / THE PROFESSOR'S PRIZE / ITCH / THE STUDENT'S FIND
Medea Norsa (1877–1952) became director of the Papyrological Institute in Florence after the death of her predecessor Girolamo Vitelli in 1935, at a time when few women were classical scholars, let alone senior figures in the field. Her house was destroyed in an Allied raid on the city in 1944 which also killed her sister, with whom she lived. After her death in 1952, a transcript of a scrap of papyrus excavated at Oxyrhynchus, which contained incomplete lines from *Myrmidons* (and had been thought lost forever in the raid), was discovered among the Institute papers.

REDACTION
John Anthony Cramer (1793–1848) was an Oxford classical scholar and later Dean of Carlisle Cathedral. His *Anecdota Parisina* collected together rare classical quotations from works in the collection of the Royal Library in Paris, including a line from Myrmidons (also found in Photius' *Lexicon*) although Cramer does not list the line's textual origin or its author. The poem also refers to the unrest in Paris during the radical uprisings of 1834 and their harsh suppression.

DRAUGHTS
The bibulous and foul-mouthed classical scholar Richard Porson (1759–1808) was born in rural Norfolk, the son of a weaver. After his studies were supported by several wealthy patrons, he was elected a Fellow at Trinity College, Cambridge, until he declined to take holy orders and so lost his stipend. Porson probably had a photographic memory, which, while useful, was also apparently a source of misery to him as 'he could never forget anything, even that he wished not to remember'. In his 1795 edition of Aeschylus, he identified a homoerotic line, quoted by Lucian's *Erotic Tales*, as a fragment of *Myrmidons*. A vivid account of Porson's life can be found in *A Gallery of Eccentrics* by Morris Bishop (1928).

HOARD
The Renaissance Sicilian scholar Giovanni Aurispa (1376–1459) scoured Constantinople for lost Greek manuscripts, incurring the wrath of the Byzantine emperor for depleting the city of its scared books. In December 1423 he brought 238 manuscripts back to Venice, including the only copy of Aeschylus' extant tragedies. It is said he was so impoverished by the mission that he had to pawn the manuscripts in order to pay their shipping costs.

THE CLERK'S CRUSADE
The siege of Constantinople during the Fourth Crusade in 1203–4 saw Christian pitted against Christian, as mutinous forces from the western or Latin church attacked the eastern city of Constantinople, drawn by its famous riches. Vivid eye-witness accounts – such as that by Niketas Akominatos – describe how, on 12th April 1204, the Latins breached the city walls by burrowing holes just big enough for single soldiers to crawl through. For three days they looted the city, destroying its Library and melting down its golden treasures to cart away. After the siege, Byzantine Greek successor states were set up in Nicaea and northern Greece where rescued works were taken for safekeeping.

GERARD'S CONSTELLATIONS
Gerard of Cremona (1114–1187) was the leading scholar at the medieval Toledo School of Translators, translating Arabic versions of Greek scientific works into Latin, making them available again to the west after they had been preserved for centuries by the Arab world. In 1175 he translated Ptolemy's *Almagest*, a Greek mathematical and astronomical treatise, and

one of the most influential scientific works of all time. Such translations were the forerunners of the rediscovery of Greek and Latin literary works during the Renaissance.

HUNAYN'S GOLD
Hunayn ibn Ishaq (809–872), an Arab Christian scholar, was known as the 'sheik of translators'. As head of the House of Wisdom in Baghdad, he translated many medical and Greek scientific works into Arabic and Syriac, particularly those of Galen (who, in turn, had quoted *Myrmidons'* proverb of an eagle shot down by a feather arrow). He followed a working method of 'sense-for-sense' rather than 'word-for-word', and was paid for his translations by weight in gold, incurring the jealous anger of wealthy court physicians.

GLOSS
Photius I (later St. Photius the Great) was a secular clerk who became Patriarch (or Pope) of Byzantium in 858 during a time of bloody religious schism in the city. As mentioned in 'Trespass', his *Lexicon* contains many rare Greek words and their usage.

AMR'S LAST WORDS
Amr ibnal-Asi (585-664), the Arab conqueror of Egypt, was also renowned as a poet and scholar. Some sources record that, on the orders of his Caliph, he destroyed any remaining secular works in the Library of Alexandria, although most of its contents had probably already been lost, bit by bit, in various incidents over the centuries, including Julius Caesar's accidental burning of the Library in 48 BCE and the Christian riots of 391 CE (see 'Diple' and 'The Christians' Cheek'). A translation of Amr's dying words can be fund in E.M. Forster's *Alexandria: A History and a Guide* (1922).

THE CHRISTIANS' CHEEK / THE PAGAN'S TIP
After their brief promotion during the reign of Julian (332–363), pagan rites were finally outlawed in 391 by the Christian emperor Theodosius. In Alexandria, bishop Theophilus and an angry mob of fellow Christians took the opportunity to attack a group of pagans who had taken refuge in the city's Serapeum – a Greek temple which had become an offshoot of the Great Library of Alexander and a centre of philosophical learning. After many street skirmishes, the Christians emerged victorious and it

is thought they then destroyed many of the precious works in the Serapeum. N.B. 'The Pagan's Tip' follows the earlier (c. 300–330) date for Palladas recently proposed by Kevin Wilkinson.

ENTRENCHMENT

In 215, the Roman emperor Caracalla (188–217) visited Alexandria on the pretence of honouring its foundation although he secretly planned to punish its citizens for their satires about him. Caracalla's revenge was not only brutal but, according to a surviving account by the ancient historian Herodian (4.8-9), reveals many chilling similarities with the actions of more modern despots, such as the creation of a walled ghetto in the city.

EROTIC TALES

Lucian of Samosata (c.125–c.200) wrote the first novels in western history, including a prototype sci-fi adventure which sees its protagonists travel to the Moon. The authorship of his dialogue *Erotes*, or 'Erotic Tales', has been questioned but the work debates the difference in heterosexual and homosexual love, concluding the latter is superior. To further the argument, various literary works are quoted including a line from *Myrmidons*, although Lucian does not mention the author and play, presumably because both were so well known at the time.

SUPPER SOPHISTRIES

Athenaeus of Naucratis (fl. c.200 CE) wrote the *Deipnosophistae* or 'Dinner Party Philosophers', an account of a lavish banquet and its guests' conversations, offering a large compendium of tales, anecdotes, facts and snippets, mostly about dining and luxurious living. In all, it cites more than 2,500 ancient works, including *Myrmidons*, making it an invaluable treasure trove of otherwise lost lines.

MARGIN

Didymus (c.63 BCE–CE 10) was an ancient Greek scholar and textual commentator who earned his nickname 'Chalcenterus' or 'Iron-guts' for the number of works he could digest. The Athenian comic playwright Aristophanes (446–386 BCE) often parodied Greek tragedies in his satires.

DIPLE

According to Plutarch's *Life* (49.3), in 48 BCE Julius Caesar was besieged in Alexandria during the civil war between the Egyptian royal family, including Cleopatra, with whom Caesar had sided. Caesar set fire to his own Roman ships in the harbour in order to stop them falling in to enemy hands – with disastrous results when flames spread across the waters to the city.

THE FERRYMAN'S ROLL

According to many sources, including Galen (Hippocrates, 3.2), Ptolemy III (246–222 BCE) was so eager to collect books for the Library at Alexandria that he ordered any found on ships in the city's harbour to be seized (and listed 'from the ships') so that new copies would be made from the manuscripts which would then be returned intact. But when Athens sent him their great tragic works, including those of Aeschylus, Ptolemy kept the originals and sent back the copies instead. The lines from *Myrmidons* quoted here are among its most impenetrable, probably referring to the burning of the Greek ships by the Trojans after Achilles' refusal to fight, and are known to us from bemused parodies in Aristophanes' plays *Frogs* and *Peace*. The poem's ferryman Charon is a fictional character but the Hellenistic poet Callimachus (310–240 BCE) did work at the Library and wrote a bibliographical survey of its works.

REVERSE

Zenon was private secretary to a ministerial advisor of the Ptolemies in the third century BCE and more than 2,000 fragments of his papers detailing accounts, bills of sale, law suits and petitions have been excavated in the rubbish tips of Oxyrhynchus. Some of the words quoted here – often attributed to *Myrmidons* – were scribbled on the back of a note sent to Zenon by one Nikarchos, a farmer, who was complaining that a business partner was not paying his share of their expenses.

SARPEDON'S VERSION

According to Plutarch (*Moralia* 841) sometime between 340 and 336 BCE, the Athenian magistrate Lycurgus ordered that all Greek tragedies, including those of Aeschylus, should be written down in definitive versions to which performances must from then on adhere. Later surviving copies might well derive from these originals. In the poem Sarpedon and his lover Diomedes are fictional but the line Sarpedon interpolates in to the text – first mentioned in 'Final Sentence' and later 'Blot' – is from one of the damaged pieces of Oxyrhnchus fragment 2256 and so could have been written in another hand.

Aeschylus' Desk

According to Lucian, Dionysius the Elder, tyrant of Syracuse (432–367 BCE), aspired to be a tragic poet and supposedly acquired Aeschylus' 'writing desk' for inspiration. His efforts were apparently atrocious although any who criticised his work were severely punished.

Thread

As seen in 'Margin', Aristophanes often poked fun at Aeschylus' complex verse in his comedies. The lines from *Myrmidons* quoted here come from Aristophanes' political satire *Assemblywomen* (*ll.* 392–3) and do not survive anywhere else. The play was first performed in 392 BCE at a time of great unrest in Athens; after the long years of the Peloponnesian War, the city had finally ceded defeat to the Spartans in 404 BCE and had then suffered an oligarchic coup which briefly dismantled its democratic constitution.

Aeschylus' Revision

Aeschylus' early work, *Persians*, draws on his experiences as a young man in defending Athens against the Persian invasion at the battle of Marathon in 490 BCE. The tyrant Hiero of Syracuse later invited Aeschylus to revive *Persians* in Sicily where, on a subsequent visit, Aeschylus is said to have died in 456 BCE. Cynaegirus is often portrayed in ancient sources as Aeschylus' brother. Herodotus (6.114) tells how he was a hero of Marathon who attempted to hold back the stern of a Persian ship with his bare hands until they were cut off by an enemy axe.

The Author

Josephine Balmer's collections include *The Word for Sorrow* (Salt, 2009 & 2013) and *Chasing Catullus: Poems, Translations & Transgressions* (Bloodaxe, 2004). Her classical translations include *Catullus: Poems of Love and Hate* (2004), *Classical Women Poets* (1996) and *Sappho: Poems & Fragments* (1984 & 1992), all published by Bloodaxe. Her study of classical translation and poetic versioning, *Piecing Together the Fragments: Translating Classical Verse, Creating Contemporary Poetry*, was published by Oxford University Press in 2013. *Letting Go: Mourning Sonnets* is forthcoming from Agenda Editions. She has written widely on poetry and translation for publications such as *The Observer*, the *Independent on Sunday*, the *Times Literary Supplement*, the *New Statesman*, and *The Times*, for which she compiles the daily Word Watch and weekly Literary Quiz. A former Chair of the Translators' Association, she was reviews editor of *Modern Poetry in Translation* from 2004-2009, and is a judge for The *Guardian*/Stephen Spender Prize for poetry translation, and an advisor to the journal, *Agenda*. She studied Classics and Ancient History at University College, London, and was awarded a PhD in Literature and Creative Writing by the University of East Anglia.

http://thepathsofsurvival.wordpress.com

Lightning Source UK Ltd.
Milton Keynes UK
UKHW03f1031140318
319416UK00002B/32/P